The Essence Of Harvard

For Peter Gibbon,
educator and thinker worthy of his alma mater.

The Essence Of Harvard

Charles W. Eliot's *Harvard Memories*

Edited and Introduced by
Paul Rich

WESTPHALIA PRESS
An imprint of Policy Studies Organization

The Essence Of Harvard:
Charles W. Eliot's *Harvard Memories*

For information:
Westphalia Press
1527 New Hampshire Ave., N.W.
Washington, D.C. 20036

ISBN-13: 978-0944285732
ISBN-10: 0944285732

Updated material and comments on this edition can be
found at the Policy Studies Organization website:
http://www.ipsonet.org

THE ESSENCE OF HARVARD:
CHARLES W. ELIOT'S *HARVARD MEMORIES*

INTRODUCTION TO THIS EDITION

Charles W. Eliot (1834-1926) was president of Harvard for forty years (1869-1909). He wrote voluminously on American education as well as on many other subjects, achieving respect as a sort of oracle on issues of the day. His imprimatur extended to the famous Five Foot Shelf, a collection of books for lifetime reading. No individual has had a more lasting influence on Harvard, and for good reason.

In *Harvard Memories* we get a succinct insight into his roots and views, and how they had a permanent influence on Harvard. His successors have never really steered the ship in another direction, though some have tried. Harvard was, he writes, always on the liberal side and "this temper among Harvard graduates has continued to the present day, and it likely to last."

President Eliot was eclectic. He had opinions on everything. He wrote inscriptions for public buildings, crusaded for public information about venereal disease, insisted on the importance of improving graduate education, and had decided views on religion. In *Memories* he has something to say about university architecture, practical and impractical, and about some now vanished Harvard buildings whose impracticalities should have been a warning to architects and college administrators.

He was taciturn, and his comments seem very reserved until one revisits them and appreciates how tongue in cheek they were. While a brief read, this volume will reward a revisit not only by Harvard alumni but also by anyone interested in the antecedents of American higher education.

Paul Rich

HARVARD MEMORIES

LONDON : HUMPHREY MILFORD

OXFORD UNIVERSITY PRESS

HARVARD MEMORIES

BY

CHARLES W. ELIOT

WITH ILLUSTRATIONS

CONTENTS

ILLUSTRATIONS

Illustrations

THE TRADITIONS OF HARVARD COLLEGE

THE TRADITIONS OF HARVARD
COLLEGE

It is a very interesting fact, I think, that Harvard College
was created by a branch of the Christian Church — the Congregational Church; the Church of Cromwell's Independents;
the Church which was most responsible for the introduction
of Cromwell's views of government into New England; the
Church which hung with intense interest on the issues of the
fighting in Europe between the Catholics and the Protestants;
the Church which issued a call for a public thanksgiving every
time they heard, months after the event, that the Protestants
had won something over the Catholics in the fluctuating fighting on the continent of Europe.

You can read on the gate close by, the gate opposite the
Unitarian Church, what the motive was for the establishment
of Harvard College. You read there that this Congregational
Church desired to breed, bring up, create in the little College, successors for the educated ministers who had come over
the Atlantic with the Massachusetts Bay Company, and had
taken charge of the Puritan settlement established in Boston in

(3)

1630. It was only six years after that date that the careful men who were at the head of the company undertook to establish a College on this spot, that ministers might be trained for the service of the people when, as it says on the gate, "our present ministers shall lie in the dust."

Now, that Congregational Church, the Established Church of Massachusetts, governed Harvard College for nearly a hundred years, with little change of purpose. Every President of Harvard College for a hundred years and more was a minister at the time of his election, except John Leverett, who had received a theological education, and was ordained a minister as soon as he was chosen President.

The first real layman was appointed President in 1829, in the second quarter of the nineteenth century. Josiah Quincy was a genuine layman, who started as a lawyer in Boston in 1793, but soon turned to public service. In politics he was a decided Federalist. He served as State Senator and Representative, and as a member of Congress, through a very critical period for the Federal party and for the country, and by his speeches and writings and through his personal energy and uprightness became a trusted leader among his contemporaries, although too independent by nature to be always an approved member of any party. He was the second Mayor of Boston

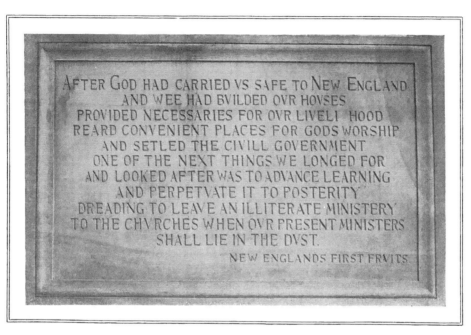

Tablet on the Johnston Gate

also, and in that office, to which he was five times reëlected, he showed large capacity for dealing with real estate and building operations, and with public finance. When he ceased to be Mayor of Boston, the Fellows of the Harvard Corporation immediately and unanimously chose him to be President of Harvard College, because they knew that a man of his quality was needed in that office. In the Board of Overseers there was, naturally, some clerical objection to this choice; but the opposition was not strong. Thence dates a new era for Harvard University.

But in addition to breeding ministers for the service of the Congregational Church, the official Church, the Established Church of Massachusetts, Harvard College began early to breed, and prepare for public functions, men who served as magistrates, teachers, social and military leaders, and heads of the communities in which they lived. Down to 1772, inclusive, the official lists of the graduates of Harvard College were arranged, like the lists of undergraduates, in an order determined by the social and occupational standing of their parents; thereafter the names were arranged in alphabetical order. The political ferment of the times accounts for this change. The lists of graduates periodically published gave the reader, down to 1890, much information about the occupations and services of the graduates. Thus italics indicated ministers, capitals governors, judges, senators, and other public servants, and italic capitals declared that the graduate had been both a minister and president of a college. The expanding service of Harvard College to the Commonwealth can be seen in these lists. From 1777 to 1887 the first ten scholars in rank had their several standings at graduation published in the official catalogues. This practice ceased in 1887, probably because the record kept by the College for each student no longer indicated his exact position in the list of his class. In the Quinquennial Catalogue for 1915 there appeared for the first time the distinctions *summa cum laude*, *magna cum laude*, and *cum laude*, printed by their initials against the names of the respective recipients.

But now, what was the predominant spirit of Harvard College while it was subject to the influence and government of a church — the Congregational Church? Always on the so-called "liberal" side, although Harvard-trained ministers differed strongly among themselves as to theological and ecclesiastical opinions. This temper among Harvard graduates has continued to the present day, and it is likely to last. They differ strongly on political, industrial, and religious questions, but have a common, unifying desire to contribute to the public welfare. Here is a Harvard tradition.

Samuel Adams

In the middle of the eighteenth century there appeared a new sort of Harvard graduate, namely, the citizen who, during the period of discussion which preceded the Revolutionary War, became an advocate of independence and was called a "patriot." Samuel Adams, who took his degree of Bachelor of Arts in 1740, delivered in 1743 a notable address, as candidate for the Master's degree, on the Commencement platform before the dignitaries of the College and the Commonwealth, on the question, "Whether it be lawful to resist the Supreme Magistrate, if the Commonwealth cannot otherwise be preserved." It prophesied his own political career and the approach of the Revolution. As the years passed, the years before the Revolutionary War broke out, more and more Harvard graduates appeared as leaders of the patriot party. Several of them became conspicuous in advocating resistance to the orders of the English Government. Samuel Adams, Joseph Warren, and James Otis spoke often in the Old South Meetinghouse in defense of the cause of freedom and independence. And this quality in Harvard graduates is recognizable from that time on — liberal, free, independent thinking in politics, society, and religion. A Harvard tradition!

When the patriot militia gathered here in Cambridge after the battle of Lexington, and proceeded to shut in the British garrison of Boston, the headquarters of their commander, General Ward, were in a house just across the way, now gone. The investment was effective from Somerville, through Cambridge by Muddy River to Boston Neck, but was ineffective on the northerly side. By June, General Ward felt strong enough to attempt to occupy one of the hills in Charlestown; and accordingly a detachment of the militia paraded in front of headquarters on the triangle of ground, just across the street here, which is still free from buildings. Before they started, on the evening of June 16, down the road to Charlestown (now Kirkland Street), Reverend Samuel Langdon, then President of Harvard College, stood before the detachment, and offered prayer on their behalf; he prayed for the inexperienced soldiers who were going to encounter veteran British regiments on Bunker's Hill the next day. This was public testimony to the fact that the Harvard College of that day was enlisted on the patriot side. Not that there were no Tories among the graduates of Harvard at this crisis — there were; but as an institution the College was enlisted on the patriot side.

In the Revolutionary period some famous graduates of Harvard signed the Declaration of Independence, many fought in the Continental Army, and served as delegates in the Continental Congress. The College was committed on the side of free-

General Ward's Headquarters

dom in political conduct, and it has remained so to this day. Another Harvard tradition!

In the meantime, the studies pursued at Harvard down to the close of the Revolutionary War had remained of the Classical type which had prevailed in the English Colleges for centuries. The students had no choice of studies, and the discipline was what we should now call strict. All the tutors — who were the chief teachers, there being in Harvard College at the end of the Revolutionary War only four professors, of whom one taught Divinity, one Hebrew and other Oriental Languages, one Mathematics and Natural Philosophy, and the fourth was just beginning to teach Anatomy and Surgery — were comparatively young men who had been brought up in the clerical and Classical tradition. The whole college course was prescribed.

This condition would look strange to you in these days, when choice of studies is ample; but to show you how recently freedom in the selection of studies came into Harvard, I can tell you about the condition of my own generation in Harvard College between 1849 and 1853. I was able to make a choice of mathematics instead of Greek in my junior year, and to carry out that preference for mathematics through my senior year; but that was the only real option I had while I was an undergraduate, about seventy years ago. In my junior year, however, I might have received elementary instruction in German or Spanish, if I had been willing to give up mathematics or Latin; and in my senior year there was a similar elusive option in Spanish, German, or Italian.

Within the first third of the nineteenth century a break occurred in this rigid system of prescribed studies in Harvard College. It resulted from a series of fortunate events, the first of which was the resort to Europe of a succession of young American Bachelors of Arts filled with ambition to carry their favorite studies quite beyond the range then accessible in Harvard or any other American college. They mostly went to Germany, and there acquired a new conception of scholarship by witnessing attainments in both teachers and students which far exceeded anything they had seen at home. They formed the opinion that selection of studies to some extent in youth was necessary to the gratification of the spirit of scholarship — necessary to it because otherwise the studies of youth remained wholly elementary. A second fortunate event was the establishment of a series of new professorships in Harvard College, the first appointments to which were made in President Kirkland's time, 1810–1828. A third event of great significance was the advent to the Corporation, or the President and Fellows, of

Five Presidents of Harvard College

QUINCY   EVERETT   SPARKS   WALKER   FELTON

thirteen men of mark and power in Massachusetts, who came into the Board, in succession and most of them for rather short terms, during President Kirkland's administration, and five of whom went on into President Quincy's. These men were all liberal-minded and far-sighted persons of large influence in eastern Massachusetts. A Divinity School and a Law School were added to the University in their time, and by their help. Under these favoring circumstances a limited but significant choice of studies was introduced into Harvard College, and was accompanied by improvement in both the volume and quality of the instruction. President Quincy steadily promoted this movement.

President Quincy, however, was followed in the presidency by three ministers, men brought up in Classical and theological studies; and the consequence was that the rudimentary elective system which was introduced under Presidents Kirkland and Quincy had almost disappeared before 1849, the year I came to College. I have already told you how very narrow the limit of choice among studies was when I was an undergraduate.

In 1860, Cornelius Conway Felton, Tutor and Professor of Greek from 1829 to 1860, a layman, was chosen President of Harvard College. He was a genial, open-minded man, whose natural gifts and practical experience lay in the direction of language and literature, but whose views of education and of the functions of a university had been much influenced by long intimacy with his next-door neighbor, Benjamin Peirce the mathematician, and with Louis Agassiz, his brother-in-law and close friend. Professor Felton was the first layman to be President of the College since 1845. Unfortunately his régime lasted but two years; for he died suddenly in office.

Then came another clerical appointee, but again a man of open mind and large nature, a man addicted to scientific pursuits in natural history and in mathematics — the Reverend Thomas Hill. He effected various advances while he was President, in respect to enlargement of the opportunities for scholarship, and he greatly encouraged in both teaching and research a group of scientific men who had been planted here, by the best of chances, for twenty or thirty years. I must name these men; because their work lay at the roots of the subsequent enlargement of the choice of studies here, and of research as a University object. They were Asa Gray, botanist — a botanist with innumerable correspondents all over the world, many of whom he had greatly obliged by sending them samples of American trees, shrubs, and herbaceous plants; and Jeffries Wyman, anatomist and physiologist, — for he combined both these fields, — a man of extraordinary scientific attainments

Asa Gray

and of the utmost freedom of mind, and desire for freedom in scientific work. Lastly, Louis Agassiz, a young Swiss savant who was brought over to this country by the Lowell Institute, and soon decided to stay here. He brought with him from Europe a great love of research and scientific adventure, and a great love of teaching. He could lecture effectively to a large audience; but his strong preference was for laboratory teaching of individuals. Under President Hill these three eminent men were advanced in university standing and in power throughout the Harvard community.

President Hill's connection with the University was but short, only seven years; for he met with fearful domestic misfortunes while here, and became himself the victim of a serious disease of the nervous system, often referred to nowadays as neurasthenia. That put an end to his career as President of Harvard. I have always been thankful that it was he who had charge of the University for the seven years preceding my election to the presidency. To give you an idea of his quality as a student of natural history — after he left Harvard and was established as minister of the Unitarian Church in Portland, Maine, he took up eagerly the observation of pests that destroyed or impaired the plants in his precious garden. One morning at dawn he established himself in a chair on one of the garden walks, and set himself to count how many insects a particular toad, with which he was familiar, would swallow before dark. There he remained till dusk, counting the prodigious number of insects which that one toad swallowed. That all-day counting was very useful in subsequent inquiries into the value of a toad as preserver of a garden. Dr. Hill advocated the enlargement throughout of the scientific teaching of the University. He also advocated enlargement of its teaching for the professions. By that time (1862) Harvard had undertaken not only a Medical School but a Theological School, a Law School, and a Scientific School, and all these professional schools had made substantial beginnings. Dr. Hill took a strong interest in them all.

On the other hand, when I was a young tutor here (1854–1858), the then President, Dr. James Walker, had absolutely no interest in any of these professional departments of the University. His entire interest was in Harvard College, the undergraduate department. He was, I think, the last President who held that view of the function of what is now called Harvard University. All those professional departments were in his view outlying things, not of the real substance of Harvard College, not for culture but for earning a livelihood. They were remote in interest, and did not deserve much attention from

Rev. Thomas Hill

either the President and Fellows or the Overseers, much less from the Faculty of Harvard College. In that respect President Walker's régime was the last of the sort.

Dr. Hill brought in another spirit. Nevertheless, to this day there are many Harvard Bachelors of Arts who hold that graduates of Harvard professional schools cannot be considered to be genuine sons of Harvard, and do not yet see that the service Harvard University renders to the country through its graduate professional schools is greater than that it renders through Harvard College proper. A Harvard tradition that is still an obstacle to progress!

I must try to give you some idea of the difficulties that attended the introduction in the eighteen-seventies and eighties of advanced studies and richer programmes, and the development of the "Elective System." There were some members of the College Faculty who thought that the President was adventuring too much in an unexplored field of liberty for students, and on insufficient pecuniary resources. They knew that, if the body of instruction in arts and sciences was to be much increased, it would have to be given by younger men than the professors, because the number of professors could not be quickly increased. They saw with alarm the increasing number of instructors and assistant professors in the College Faculty.

Were they equal to the new work asked of them? Were not young men coming to Harvard for a "a good time," or for social objects, or for athletics, and not for hard intellectual work of any sort? How can a young man of eighteen know what he had better study?

The professor of surgery, who at that time had complete charge of the Harvard Medical School, went round to all the members of the Board of Overseers — he was a man of quick wit, picturesque language, and great personal influence — and told them that this young President was going to wreck the Harvard Medical School: it would cease to exist in a year or two, if his revolutionary reconstruction of the School were allowed. "He actually proposes," said this professor, "to have written examinations for the degree of doctor of medicine. I had to tell him that he knew nothing about the quality of the Harvard medical students; more than half of them can barely write. Of course they can't pass written examinations." Dr. Bigelow's observation of the quality of the then medical student was somewhat exaggerated, but not grossly so. Nevertheless, the Board of Overseers ultimately adopted the proposition for reform in the Medical School which came to them from the President and Fellows. And yet that adoption was due at the moment to one unforeseen happening. I like to tell this kind

Charles Francis Adams

of story; for it illustrates the unpredictable terms and conditions of progress in educational matters and in human society.

The Overseers had debated for three meetings this proposed conversion of the Medical School into a school in which the instruction should be progressive through each year of the course, and should run through nine months of each year, instead of through four only. It was further proposed that no candidate should obtain his degree unless he had passed a strict examination in all the chief departments of instruction, instead of five out of nine as had previously been the requirement.

The hour of taking the final vote on the acceptance of this plan by the Board of Overseers approached, when suddenly Mr. Charles Francis Adams, who had recently returned from rendering a very great service as Minister to England from the United States during the Civil War, said to me, "Whom shall I put into the Chair?" — he was President of the Board of Overseers — "I wish to speak." I had not the faintest idea on which side of the hot debate Mr. Adams was going to speak. He had uttered no word during the three meetings which had already been devoted to it. But he soon stepped out on the floor, and as he began to speak, it was evident that he was much stirred. There was a fierce glare in his eyes, and his face grew red as he told this story:

"I think it is high time that the Harvard Medical School should be fundamentally changed. A young graduate of the Harvard Medical School established himself in my town of Quincy a year or two ago, and was getting along quite well in practice. But one day it was observed that an Irish laborer, to whom he had been called, died suddenly, and unexpectedly to his family. Nothing was done about it, for the family did not pursue the subject. Then another laborer, a granite-cutter in Quincy, suddenly died under this young man's care; but again nothing came of it. One day the wife of an American mechanic saw her husband, who had not appeared to her to be very sick, suddenly become comatose; and in great alarm she told the young doctor that she wanted an older physician. The oldest physician in Quincy was called in; and when he looked at the patient he said to the young physician, 'What have you done for him?' To which the young physician replied frankly, 'I have given him so much sulphate of morphia.' 'Well, doctor,' the older man replied, 'you have killed him' — which turned out to be the case."

Mr. Adams told this story and added, "Now, I suppose this young doctor was one of those graduates of the Harvard Medical School who were required to pass only five examinations out of nine to obtain the degree. I am in favor of the proposition which has come to us from the Corporation." The vote was taken almost immediately, and there was a strong majority in favor of reform in the School. Till that moment I had not felt sure that there would be any majority for it.

I have told you this story because it illustrates perfectly the uncertainties which attend all reform movements, no matter whether in education or in government. Sometimes it seems as if the achievement of a great reform had been, after all, a matter of chance or accident. You will find many people saying so at this moment about the reform in our country called prohibition; whereas prohibition has been more than twenty-five years in coming, and the steps have been gradual, until the War prohibition law, enacted for the protection of the encampments of our soldiers who were preparing to go to the battlefields of France, caused a sudden burst of public opinion in its favor.

Lovers of the "good old times," and believers in driving children and youth rather than leading them, and in mental "discipline," particularly if disagreeable, rather than in mental delights, sometimes ask me: "How in the world did Harvard College turn out such remarkable scholars, poets, and historians in the old days, when there was no elective system at all, no opportunity in the College for any advanced studies?"

The answer is simple, and it is illustrated by many of the

historians, poets, authors, and scientists of the older time, particularly from the beginning of the nineteenth century to the middle of it. The old régime gave them a great deal of leisure, and that leisure they used in their own way, in following whatever studies they loved. Hence life-long scholarship and authorship.

The original Harvard College was wonderfully small — a little group of tutors and students. If you look over the Quinquennial Catalogue, in which the successive classes of graduates of Harvard College are recorded, you will find that no class numbered ten until 1659; that no class reached twenty until 1690 and 1695, each of which numbered twenty-two; and that the College was over eighty years old before it graduated a class numbering forty or more; and that this happened only twice down to 1762. The class that contained Samuel Adams and Samuel Langdon numbered only twenty-two at graduation. The class that I joined as a freshman in the fall of 1849 was the largest the College had ever had, numbering eighty-seven. Dismissals being rare, and admissions to advanced standing more numerous, the class numbered ninety at graduation — a number first attained two hundred and thirteen years after the first class graduated with nine members. The professional schools also were very small.

One striking phenomenon of the last fifty years has been the large growth in the number of students of this institution, graduate and undergraduate. But nobody who has been much interested in the conduct of Harvard University has ever paid much attention to numbers. Indeed, to effect the necessary reforms of 1870 to 1890 repeatedly required taking large risks as to numbers. Dr. Bigelow said in 1870 that this young President would kill off the Medical School in a few years; and indeed the Medical School did have a serious decrease in the number of students in the first years of the reform. The same thing happened in the Law School. Dean Langdell and I watched anxiously the declining numbers of law students when the Case System was adopted by the School. It took several years to recover from that decline; but when the early graduates of the Law School under the Langdell system got out into the world and made a name for themselves, so that the merits of the system began to be recognized by the Bar, the number of law students began gradually to increase; and in spite of higher standards of admission, longer residence, and stricter requirements for the degree, the School has had for many years quite as many students as it wants.

Nobody now accepts numbers as conclusive evidence of the prosperity of any of the several divisions of an American university. It all depends on what kinds of students are admitted to the institution. Columbia University, for example, has an enormous number of students who are admitted to the summer schools, and other thousands who come in for short courses. Any university which desires to increase the number of students on its rolls can easily do so under the title University Extension. Never be guided by the number of students in a school or university in judging its quality.

Now, what is the traditional spirit of Harvard University? I should describe it as a spirit of service — not necessarily in what we call public service, but a spirit of service in all the professions, both learned and scientific, including business; a desire, a firm purpose, to be of use to one's fellow men. And that spirit governs in all wholesome fields of human activity. It is just the same in the Law School and the Medical School that it is in the College proper; and I may add, it is the same to-day that it was at the time of the Civil War. I see no difference between then and now in the spirit of the young men — in the nature of their resolutions concerning their life-careers. I do see some difference in their reflections about what they call socialization. I see some difference in their views about the halting progress of democracy. For me democracy simply means freedom for each individual to arrange his training and his life-career so that he

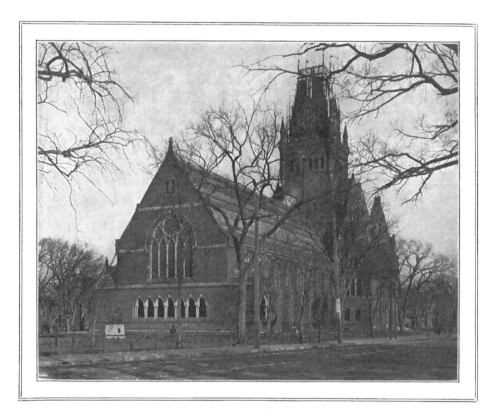

Memorial Hall

can do his best for the common welfare. You all understand that the variety of human nature is such that one man's best is very different from another's, just as one man's mental habits and powers are different from every other's. With these varieties in human nature democracy has to deal; and the hopes of democracy depend on whether all these varieties are developed and made serviceable.

James Russell Lowell said in his noble address at the two hundred and fiftieth anniversary of the founding of Harvard College: "Democracy must show its capacity for producing, not a higher average man, but the highest possible types of manhood in all its manifold varieties, or it is a failure." I am sorry he added "or it is a failure"; for that failure should never be contemplated. Doubtless Lowell meant to intimate that very high types of human nature had appeared under earlier forms of government and society, and that democracy must equal and, indeed, surpass the older forms in this respect. I think that that is the general belief of Harvard men; and to me it is one of the most characteristic of their beliefs. But if I were to be called upon to define in a single phrase the traditional and the present spirit of Harvard University, I should say that it was and is the spirit of service.

THE FUNCTION OF A UNIVERSITY

THE FUNCTION OF A UNIVERSITY

THE function of a university is, of course, a subject that I
have had occasion to think about a good deal in the course of
my life; and I have personally seen the functions of most universities in the world change since I first became connected
with Harvard University. That is true all over the Occidental
world — in Germany, in England, in France, in Italy, and in
our own country.

The university in all times has been primarily a society of
scholars, of men who were actuated by a love of study and re-
flection, of experiment, and of reaching out for the facts of all
nature, including man, and who found delight in associating
with men of like mind, their fellows in the university. In the
universities which started in Europe completely under direction
of the Catholic Church, or of the Greek Church, there was another motive, to be sure, namely, the purpose to work for the
benefit of the Church, the purpose to further its interests as a
divine and human organization, an ecclesiastical power. But
more than a hundred years ago this motive practically ceased
to exist in the universities of both Europe and America; and

particularly here in Harvard that religious or church motive, which was, of course, the principal motive for the foundation of the College, ceased. That ecclesiastical or church motive in Harvard College lasted for nearly two hundred years; so that almost all the tutors, and all the presidents down to 1829 (with one partial exception) were ministers. The tutors, to be sure, were sometimes young men who were preparing to be ministers, but had not yet attained to the ministry. Hence the curriculum for Harvard students was composed chiefly of Classical and Biblical subjects.

About the middle of the eighteenth century there appeared a striking change in the product of Harvard College, which turned out to be of the first importance, the beginning, indeed, of the secular functions which have now become its chief object. The College began to produce a considerable proportion of young men who became leaders in business, law, medicine, politics, and society; men who possessed in youth, or acquired later through reading and experience, knowledge, imagination, and enterprise. The names of Samuel Adams, Isaac Hinckley, Edward Winslow, Foster Hutchinson, Samuel Cooper, James Otis, Thomas Cushing, James Bowdoin, Thomas Bulfinch, Edward Augustus Holyoke, Samuel Moody, William Ellery, Ebenezer Storer, Artemas Ward, Robert Treat Paine, and

Oliver Prescott, all of whom graduated between 1740 and 1750, illustrate this function of Harvard College. Anyone who is familiar with. the Harvard Quinquennial Catalogue and with colonial history between 1740 and 1790 can easily add to this significant list.

Another stage in the development of Harvard College into a university came much later, namely, the beginning in 1782 of attention at Harvard to preparing young men for the professions. I suppose that evolution to be the most serious change which the old Harvard College has come through. It began with the first attempts on the part of a few physicians and friends of theirs to provide at Harvard College instruction suitable for young men who meant to be physicians or surgeons. That was the beginning here of what we call professional training.

The next effort was to prepare men whose desire was to enter the profession of law. The Law School dates from the year 1817, and the Theological School from about the same time. All along from 1636 down, Harvard College itself had been regarded as a school for the preparation of ministers; but early in the nineteenth century a group of persons who had ceased to believe the Calvinistic dogmas of the original Established Church of Massachusetts set about building up in Harvard

University a theological school in which "no assent to the peculiarities of any denomination of Christians shall be required either of the instructors or of the students." That was the third of the professions to obtain what may be called official connection with the University. So three professional schools had been well begun before the accession of Josiah Quincy to the Presidency.

President Quincy was the first real layman to be made President of the College. His selection indicated a fundamental change of mind among the actual Governors of the College as to the kind of man that had better be made President. President Quincy had had no connection whatever with the clerical profession. He was a man of property and a business man of large capacity. He had had long experience as a legislator and executive, as I have said on an earlier page, and everywhere had shown himself an energetic, independent, and faithful public servant. These were the qualities which the then Governors of Harvard College thought were needed in the Presidency. Naturally, President Quincy took a strong interest in the young Law School, in which his intimate friend Joseph Story, a Justice of the Supreme Court of the United States, had just accepted the Dane Professorship of Law. Judge Story held this professorship for sixteen years and gave a large part of his time to

Josiah Quincy

its work. How times have changed for the Justices of the Supreme Court during the past hundred years you may learn by comparing Judge Story's freedom to live and work in Cambridge with the close confinement in Washington, except in midsummer, of the two Harvard Justices on that Court now, Holmes and Brandeis.

Judge Story's first plan was to build a Law School for Bachelors of Arts and persons of equivalent training; but he soon found that policy impracticable, and accepted all sorts of candidates for admission; so that the student body became heterogeneous as regards previous education, and remained so for more than fifty years. Attendance for eighteen months was the only requirement for the degree.

President Quincy liked to get up early, and go to work. Professor Story did not. One bright day the President attended a lecture by Professor Story, and took a chair on the platform behind him. After a time, the Professor noticed that his usually attentive class was tittering. Glancing behind, he saw the President fast asleep. Without any change of voice or manner he remarked: "Gentlemen, you see before you an illustration of the deplorable consequences of early rising." The coöperative labors of these two distinguished men for Harvard University covered a period of sixteen pregnant years; for Story was a

Fellow from 1825 to his death in 1845, while Quincy was President from 1829 to 1845.

While Dr. John Thornton Kirkland, an admirable preacher and great social favorite, was President (1810–1828) and John Davis was Treasurer (1810–1827), the management of the property and accounts of Harvard College was less efficient and exact than it had usually been. The President and Fellows between 1630 and 1810 had brought the College safely through a series of wars, paper-money periods, commercial panics, the Revolution, and the first twenty years of the Constitution, and were naturally proud of this record. The election of Ebenezer Francis, a competent and successful man of business, as Treasurer, in 1827, determined a quick reform in the business methods of the Corporation; and the advent of President Quincy in 1829 confirmed and perfected that reform.

During the Presidency of Dr. Kirkland no less than seven new professorships were founded in Harvard College; and five of these were filled, in spite of the fact that not one of the seven had an endowment sufficient to provide a full salary for the Professor appointed. Among these five was the Smith Professorship of the French and Spanish Languages and Literatures, to which George Ticknor, later the historian of Spanish Literature, was appointed in 1817. Professor Ticknor, after

Judge Joseph Story

graduating at Dartmouth in 1807, had travelled and studied for some years in Europe, and had made the acquaintance of eminent scholars and authors in several European countries. He had formed the opinion that the study of modern languages should be added to the prevailing programme of academic studies in the United States; and he made that introduction his immediate object as professor in Harvard College. These studies, however, could not be prescribed for all students. Here began the provision of elective studies at Harvard. President Quincy heartily believed in the provision of some elective studies, and warmly supported throughout his administration this enlargement of the instruction offered.

As a structure Harvard College was now coming to look a little more like a university as understood on the Continent of Europe, and the conception of a university as a society of scholars — teachers and students together — had entered the minds of many Harvard men. Of course, by that time the German universities had already become seats of advanced study and teaching; and it was in Germany that a few young American Bachelors of Arts, bound on educational adventure, caught a glimpse of what advanced scholarship meant in the direction of teaching, or authorship, or research.

At that time (1817–1867) a young man of any capacity at all

could accomplish all the prescribed tasks of a day, including the attendance at recitations, in a small number of hours. Four hours were for a bright fellow the utmost that would be needed; and three of those would be attendance at recitations. In consequence, young men like George Bancroft, Ralph Waldo Emerson, Frederic H. Hedge, Francis Parkman, and Charles Eliot Norton, got their education and developed their tastes for study and research, not at all within the system and curriculum of Harvard College, but through spending their ample leisure on studies that they loved. They followed their bent, in short, unimpeded. That was conspicuously the case in the "education" of Ralph Waldo Emerson. He was an omnivorous reader, and an observant and reflective wanderer in woods and by-ways. He worked on the things that interested him, with companions of his choice, and college duties obstructed him hardly at all.

In 1850–1853, I illustrated the same condition of things in Harvard College. From the middle of my freshman year till the end of my senior year I had, by favor of Professor Josiah P. Cooke, opportunities to study chemistry and mineralogy which no other undergraduate enjoyed; for I was made free of Professor Cooke's private laboratory and of the Mineral Cabinet of which he had charge. I also accompanied him on his

George Ticknor

visits to mineral localities and mining and metallurgical works. As I enjoyed very much these laboratory and field studies, I naturally gave a large part of my time to them. Nevertheless I stood well in my regular college work in all four years, there being time enough for both the compulsory and the chosen tasks, if one were diligent.

Down to 1845 the professorships in Harvard College endowed by individual benefactors were all on theology, morals, law, language, literature, history, or philosophy, except the Hollis Professorship of Mathematics and Natural Philosophy (1727), three on medical subjects, anatomy, physic, and materia medica (1791), one — the remarkable Rumford Professorship — on the Application of Science to the Useful Arts, and one on natural history (1842). About 1845 a few men connected with the Governing Boards of Harvard University, or the College Faculty, began to study the means of creating a body of systematic instruction in physical and exact science and its applications in mining, manufacturing, and agriculture; and in support of this project Abbott Lawrence of Boston — a great mill-owner, interested especially in the manufacture of cotton goods — came forward with generous gifts. He had learned by observation that the mills at Lowell needed great engineering works to establish their water-power securely. He observed the same thing at Lawrence later. He had come to see that men skilled in engineering and chemistry were necessary to the successful prosecution of American manufacturing in many lines. He also saw that in bleacheries and printworks many chemicals and elaborate chemical processes were needed. Accordingly he founded here a Scientific School (later called by his name), built its first building, equipped therein an excellent chemical laboratory, and endowed a professorship in engineering. That was a great step toward the development of seventeenth-century Harvard College into a modern university.

The tendency to provide for applied science at the University has increased as time has gone on. From 1850 to 1920 inclusive, fifty-two endowed professorships were established in Harvard University, of which thirty-six were devoted to applied science, if political economy, economics, and banking be considered applications of science. With the establishment of the Scientific School there came a great enlargement of expenditures in the University on museums and collections. Professor Asa Gray had been making his Herbarium for some years, but it was his own work and his own property; the Mineral Cabinet had also become valuable, and that was the property of Harvard College. In 1847 new expenditures began on collections in natural history, to which Mr. Lawrence and

The Botanic Garden of Harvard University

other private benefactors contributed. In 1857 the Museum of Comparative Zoölogy was founded, and in 1866 the Peabody Museum. Later came the Semitic Museum, the Fogg Art Museum, the Germanic Museum, and the Social Museum, all originally works of private benefaction, but involving also large university expenditures.

A small group of great scholars in the sciences had an important share in this movement. Asa Gray, for many years the leading botanist of the United States, built up in his Herbarium and in the Botanic Garden a body of advanced instruction which gradually supplied to the country a considerable group of botanical specialists who not only held important posts in other colleges and universities, but advanced botanical science in America. He also started the first Summer School ever held at Harvard, or indeed in the United States, his argument for the summer course being that summer was the time of year when botany could best be studied by interested persons, either men or women.

Jeffries Wyman, anatomist and physiologist, led the way in offering throughout the year, in his laboratory in Boylston Hall, and later in the Peabody Museum, advanced laboratory instruction for a few students whom he personally selected, or who were directed to him by medical or scientific friends.

In the eighteen-seventies and eighties a series of well-trained specialists went out into the medical and scientific professions from Professor Wyman's laboratory.

Louis Agassiz brought hither from the University at Neufchâtel great attainments in the study of glacial phenomena in the Swiss mountains, with enthusiasm for the teaching of the natural sciences, both in their elements and in their highest reaches, and especial zeal in training advanced students by the laboratory and field method. His method of teaching had many novel features for us at Harvard. You may perhaps get some conception of it from the following anecdote.

The instruction given in the Harvard Medical School in 1871–1874 was still extremely elementary, although it had already begun to improve. William Sturgis Bigelow, son of the eminent surgeon, Henry J. Bigelow, went through the Medical School between 1871 and 1874, but at graduation was not sure that he wished to be a doctor or a surgeon. One day he said to his father: "I want to study some more natural history before I decide to be a practising physician. I want to go to Professor Agassiz's laboratory and study under him." His father thought that the son's scheme was foolish, but that he had better try it. So young Bigelow forthwith entered Professor Agassiz's laboratory. On the first day there Agassiz gave him a trilobite and

Louis Agassiz

said to him: "Look carefully at this trilobite, and describe in this notebook everything you can see on that fossil." He said nothing more; and young Bigelow worked all the morning on those directions. In the afternoon Agassiz appeared again at Bigelow's desk, and remarked: "That's pretty good so far; but you have n't finished by any means. Go right on." Young Bigelow put in all the afternoon. The next morning Agassiz came in again and remarked: "Bigelow, you are getting on. Keep right at it."

When Friday evening came, young Bigelow went home to his father's house. In answer to the question: "What have you been doing in Agassiz's laboratory?" the young man described the process he had been through. "What," said Dr. Bigelow, "no book!" — "None." — "No instruction?" — "None." — "Nothing else said?" — "Nothing." — "Nothing to guide you, no sketch or anything?" — "Nothing." — "Well," said the father, "that is exactly the way a puppy has to learn how to live and get his living." True, but he should have added, that what a puppy learns he learns very well, and that the teaching method which Agassiz followed is the only way to teach thoroughly any natural science.

In all departments of the University a careful observation of actual facts, an accurate recording of the facts determined, and a just and limited inference from the recorded facts have come to be the primary methods of study and research.

Just before the Civil War the structure of Harvard University as a group of professional schools on top of the College became clearly visible. Harvard had already attained at that time something which neither Oxford nor Cambridge had then reached. Indeed, Oxford and Cambridge have scarcely developed to-day a complete recognition of professional schools as an indispensable part of a university, although considerable changes are at this moment in progress there.

There succeeded to President Quincy a series of presidents who had little interest in any of the professional schools. They were all ministers by training. Presidents Everett, Sparks, and Walker had very scanty interest in the infant elective system in Harvard College. President Walker took no interest in the Harvard Divinity School, although he received there his own professional education. When I first began to work as a tutor in mathematics in Harvard College under an appointment made by President Walker, he and Mrs. Walker invited me to take supper with them every Friday evening. Their own supper was habitually so very simple and scanty, that Mrs. Walker informed me that I should be provided with an additional dish; but this additional dish was usually only

Dr. Henry J. Bigelow

some form of preserved fruit, like stewed quince, for example. After supper Dr. Walker often showed me the votes that he was preparing for the Corporation meeting the next day. A considerable proportion of these votes were not related to any measures for the benefit of Harvard College, but were votes which Dr. Walker had undertaken to prepare in the interest of the professional schools, representatives of which had been explaining to him their desires. I took much more interest than President Walker did in these votes about professional school matters; but the votes were of course written out by the President with conscientious care, ready for the action of the Corporation. Fifteen years later when I remarked, at the first meeting of the Corporation which I attended as President, that I had no further business, every member of the Board jumped from his seat and rushed into the ante-room, leaving me alone at the table. They were all of them about twice my age, and had known my father and mother and many friends of theirs. After some minutes Treasurer Silsbee came back alone from the ante-room and said: "Mr. President, the Fellows in the next room are very much pleased with the manner in which you conducted this meeting. You have done exactly what Dr. James Walker used to do when he was President."

From 1869 to 1909 the President of Harvard University

took quite as much interest in reforms and improvements in the Harvard professional schools as he did in the reconstruction of Harvard College.

In 1908 a small group of professors of economics and kindred subjects began to study, at the instance of the President, the organization of the School which ultimately was called the Graduate School of Business Administration. All along Harvard College had produced among its Bachelors of Arts young men who went out into business, largely into businesses which required in good measure knowledge of applied science, of sound business administration, and of the wise and considerate management of the working force; but it could hardly be said that it was a distinct object in the University to train men for business. Now it has become so. In addition to the Department of Economics in the Faculty of Arts and Sciences a special School of Business Administration was created in 1909. This School of Business Administration was promptly copied in various other institutions, some of which are commercial rather than educational; and as a result there will hereafter be many more well-trained business men in the country than there used to be.

In respect to the teaching of political economy, or economics, I can perhaps give you some notion of the great change which

Francis Bowen

has taken place since 1869 by describing the work done by Professor Francis Bowen, the only Harvard professor who then dealt at all with the subject of political economy. He gave only about a quarter of his time to that subject, because he had so many other subjects to deal with. His idea of teaching political economy was to write an elementary book on the subject, and to require the senior class — it was a required subject of the senior year — to read that book. He gave no lectures; he sometimes commented upon those pages of the book which had been assigned as the lesson of the day, to be repeated in the recitation room by those students who had studied the lesson. It is a long way from that condition of things to the present organization of the Department of Economics.

There is another aspect of a university as a society of scholars about which I wish to say a word. It should be a society of teachers and students, a real comradeship in scholarly adventures, no matter what subject the group may be pursuing. That intimate comradeship involves small use of the lecture method and large use of the small-class method, where the intercourse between teacher and student is conversational, intimate, and stimulating to all participants.

The kind of companionship which obtains among the students of a university is of great importance to the realization

of the university as a society of scholars. To know by name
and pat on the back two hundred men is not much of an object;
but to know a few men body and soul, and to have sympathetic
intercourse with these few, is a large part of what a university
can do for youth. At the English colleges the serious students
who have scholarly ambition divide themselves rather promptly
into small groups, who, it may be, pay the same tutor during
term time, or resort to the same professor or scholar all through
the long vacation. They thus acquire a few friendships that
have a strong influence on their future lives. You will find a
very good example of that kind of intimacy in the account
that William E. Gladstone gave of his friendship with Arthur
Hallam. That friendship influenced profoundly the whole of
Gladstone's mode of thought and future career.

THE HARVARD YARD AND BUILDINGS

THE HARVARD YARD AND BUILDINGS

I FIRST became well acquainted with the grounds and buildings of Harvard College in 1849, when I came hither as a Freshman; but I had previously learned a good deal about them, because my father, Samuel A. Eliot (Harvard A.B. 1817), who was Treasurer of Harvard University from 1842 to 1853, printed in 1848 a small book which he called "A Sketch of the History of Harvard College." It was a work of much care and pains, but brief so far as the text went. In the appendix he added, first, a list of all the grants — some of which were for land and buildings, but most of them in money — from the Massachusetts Legislature from the beginning down to 1814, covering a period of 178 years (1636–1814). Then he added an even more interesting list — very nearly complete in all probability, but not guaranteed complete — of all the private gifts — books, utensils, or endowments for current use — made to the President and Fellows of Harvard College from the beginning down to 1845. In these lists I took a special interest — I hardly know why, for I was only thirteen years old. Lastly, this appendix contained a plan or chart of what we now call the College Yard, with the enclosing streets; and that plan or chart also interested me very much indeed; so that I really knew a good deal about the grounds of Harvard College when I came here as a Freshman in 1849. And I knew in fact some things about the College estate in Cambridge which were not on the plan of the College enclosure in my father's sketch of the history of Harvard. I knew about the acquirement of the Observatory lot, and of the Botanic Garden, then much smaller than it is now, but containing the residence and the collections of Asa Gray.

PLAN OF HARVARD UNIVERSITY
1850, 1875, 1907

Now we will begin with a plan which exhibits on one sheet the grounds and buildings at three different dates — 1850, 1875, and 1907. This is the whole development during fifty-seven years. You see there are three groups of buildings: the dark-colored ones, which are the earlier buildings; then some inclosed by black lines, which are those added between 1850 and 1875; and lastly the more numerous recent additions. This drawing shows at once how few the buildings existing in 1850 were in comparison with the structures now belonging to Harvard University; and yet this plan, as you see, does not extend across the river or go as far west as the Botanic Garden and the Observatory.

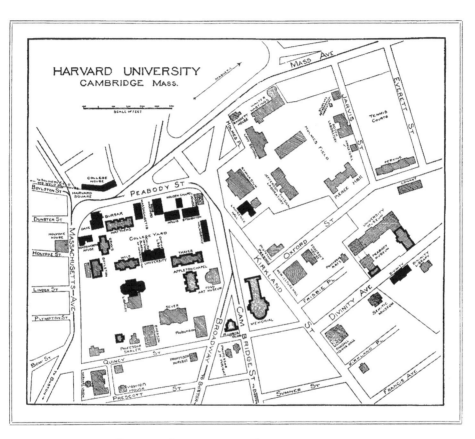

Plan of Harvard University

HARVARD YARD, 1848

THIS is the view of the Yard of 1848, which was printed in my father's "Sketch of the History of Harvard College." It was his object, among other things, to show the way in which this block of land was slowly acquired through different gifts and purchases; and you see here the names of the sellers or givers of these various lots of land which finally in 1848 made up the College Yard. You see that many of them were bought from families which had long been settled here in Cambridge, as, for instance, the Wigglesworth lot, which was formerly owned by Professor Wigglesworth of the eighteenth century; and here are two other old Cambridge names — Goffe and Betts. The piece which is described as a town grant is close to the original buildings, but they did not stand on it; it was later acquired. The picture shows Massachusetts Hall, Harvard Hall, and a representation of the first Stoughton Hall. The latter was a short-lived building, though built of brick; in fact, it was so badly constructed that it had to be taken down because it was falling down. It remains true that for pleasant aspect and

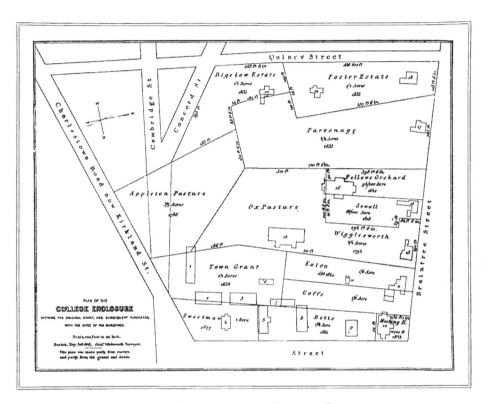

The Harvard Yard

1848

good proportions the earliest buildings here were the best. I refer, of course, to Massachusetts, Harvard, and Hollis; and Holden was another instance of very pleasing design. Hollis remains to this day the best-looking of the College buildings, the most agreeable from the architect's point of view. That, I suppose, is the reason why, when Mr. Charles A. Coolidge, the present Consultant in Architecture, came to design Perkins Hall on Oxford Street, he used Hollis as his type, so to speak, although Perkins is twice as big as Hollis.

You will notice on this map a lot called the meeting-house addition to the College Yard. It was not considerable in area but it had a commanding position. When the First Church in Cambridge, now represented by the church opposite the principal College Gate, abandoned its church on this lot, the College bought the land. You will see here, too, the site of Wadsworth House. That was a building of great merit. In my eyes, it is still one of the best-looking of the College buildings. It was built for President Wadsworth by the Colonial Government — by Massachusetts, that is to say. It has undergone many alterations during the last eighty years, but still remains, architecturally, a very pleasing building.

PLAN OF HARVARD YARD, 1857

THE next is a quite different piece of work on the part of three undergraduates in the academic year 1856–57, while I was a tutor teaching Sophomore prescribed Mathematics. I was appointed tutor in the spring of 1854; and my friend and classmate James M. Peirce, having been appointed tutor in Mathematics by the Corporation a week earlier than I, had the choice of the Freshman or the Sophomore class for the coming academic year. He chose the Freshman, and I was obliged to teach the Sophomore Class, later, of course, the Class of 1857. I had some rather important subjects of instruction that year for a youth of twenty who had never taught at all. I had the advanced algebra, the trigonometry, and the analytic geometry. When I came to the teaching of trigonometry, I found it very distasteful to teach it without any field-work, any use of instruments, or any practice in measuring lines and angles or in draughting; and yet it was manifestly impossible to provide such instruction for the whole class, which numbered about seventy.

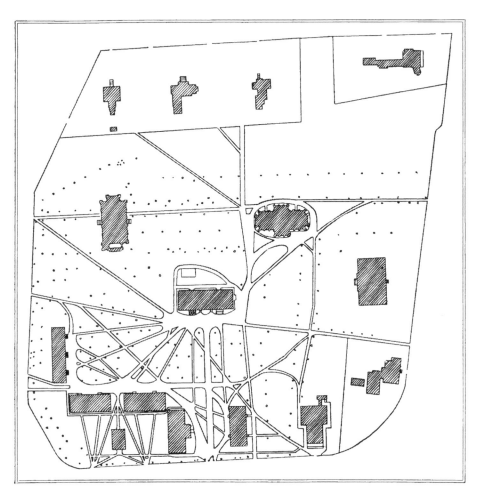

Map of the College Yard
1856–57

The Harvard Yard and Buildings

In studying chemistry and mineralogy from 1850 to 1853, in Professor Cooke's private laboratory and the Harvard Mineral Cabinet, — the only undergraduate in Harvard College to have such privileges, — I had learned that work in laboratory and field was the only satisfactory way to study science. In 1855–56, when I again had charge of Sophomore Mathematics, — the class subsequently known as the Class of 1858, — I ventured upon a new experiment in contemporary Harvard teaching of a prescribed subject. I collected, with some difficulty, surveying instruments enough to offer instruction in surveying to volunteers from the class. Somewhat to my surprise, about fifteen men volunteered to take this field-work in trigonometry. This group surveyed with great care the College Yard; and on this you will see, in the first place all the paths indicated, all the buildings, of course, and also all the trees. Every tree was placed by these young surveyors and put into this drawing. The same group also mapped the streets of Cambridge within a mile of University Hall. The three students who did most of this work were McKenzie, Stickney, and Lathrop, all three high scholars. It always gave Alexander McKenzie, minister of the Congregational Church here in Cambridge at the corner of Mason and Garden Streets, great satisfaction in after life to recall his contribution to this undertaking. Lathrop was first a teacher and then a lawyer. Albert Stickney had a distinguished career at the New York Bar. No one of them followed a profession in which mathematics or surveying came into play. This excellent map was originally colored with a strong green for the grass, and another tint for the buildings. It contains Boylston Hall and Appleton Chapel, which were not completed at the time. It contains also the Gore Hall of former days, which has now completely disappeared. This was the entire group of buildings within the Yard in 1856.

HARVARD SQUARE IN 1858

THE picture is next Harvard Square. You see it has the look of a country village; that is just the way it did look, like the headquarters of a country village.

One of my aunts, Eliot aunts, married Professor Andrews Norton (Harvard A.B., 1804); and my father, when his sister was engaged to Mr. Norton, had just got home from Europe, where he had made "the grand tour." His father, Samuel Eliot, was a rich merchant who kept what Yankees used to call a "variety store" on Dock Square in Boston; but it somewhat resembled, on a small scale, the present department stores like Filene's, and Hovey's, and Jordan-Marsh's, because he kept for sale everything available at that day. He imported most of the goods he sold, as they were not then made in this country. In this business he made a great deal of money; so that he could well afford to keep his son Samuel in Europe for two years, just studying French, German, and Italian, visiting universities, parks, gardens, museums, and famous works of art and architecture, and travelling from place to place in his own carriage.

When the young man returned to Boston, his father almost immediately told him he had bought a house and some land for Catherine in Cambridge, northeast of the College and Divinity Hall. The old gentleman, who had a beautiful house at the corner of Beacon and Tremont Streets in Boston, with a garden which ran back to Somerset Street, also said: "But it does not look to me like a gentleman's house. It is not a gentleman's house and place. I want you to make it into a proper residence for your sister Catherine who is to be married to Professor Norton." My father proceeded to execute this order thoroughly, having great interest in such work. First he faced the house the other way. It had faced north, toward Somerville. He made the principal entrance on the south side of the house, and put two bows on that front, which are there still. It had been approached from the Somerville side, but ever since my father made the new avenue it has been approached from Kirkland Street (the Charlestown road). You can imagine how bare the place was of trees; for my aunt told me that when she was first married she could sit at her chamber window and see anybody coming in at the gate of the avenue on Kirkland Street, there being nothing in the way. Some of us have been in the habit for many years of talking about "Norton's Woods." Now, it was my father who planted all those trees,

Harvard Square in 1858

both evergreen and deciduous. So landscape architects can look forward to having new plantations, made next year or five years hence, come to be regarded, even within a single generation, as natural forests.

A large family was born to Mr. and Mrs. Andrews Norton; and the children grew to maturity in that house, now owned by Professor Sachs. They were first cousins of mine, and I went there a great deal as boy and man. That family invariably, if they were going down to this area,—Harvard Square,—said, "I am going to the village." That was the only expression that they ever used to indicate what we now call "Harvard Square"; one of those daughters is still living, and remembers distinctly this family usage. It prevailed in other Old Cambridge families.

We see some rather amusing things in this picture. The hay-scales were then a principal feature of Harvard Square, important because the surrounding farmers were in the habit of bringing their loads of hay to this point to be weighed; and there was a public weigher provided for that express purpose. Two horse-cars may be seen standing there. They were, at the time this photograph was taken, a recent introduction. Horse-cars! Laying the tracks had been a noteworthy enterprise; and for some time they ended at the corner of West Boston Bridge and Charles Street, Boston. There you left the car, and walked the rest of the way to your destination in Boston.

Those horse-cars call to my mind that all the conveyance of passengers between Cambridge and Boston when I came to College, and a good deal later, was performed by vehicles called "busses." There were four-horse busses, which started from Harvard Square, followed Main Street, and drove as far as Brattle Street in Boston. There were also supplementary two-horse busses, smaller and lighter. What did that method of communication between Cambridge and Boston mean? It meant that the riders in these busses were, as a rule, a few professional men who lived in Cambridge and had their offices in Boston; or, in the middle of the day, some adventurous ladies who preferred to do some of their shopping in Boston rather than in Cambridge stores. All the work was done by these busses — with two or four horses — going once in half an hour or so between the two towns.

When I was in College (1849–53), my parents lived on Beacon Street, Boston, at the top of the hill; and I always went home to that house for Saturday afternoons and Sundays. What were the means of conveyance from Boston to Harvard Square on Sunday evening? Only one two-horse bus, which started from Brattle Street, Boston, at eight o'clock and held about twelve persons inside. The time between father's house and my College room was nearly an hour by that route. On a rainy night the one omnibus might be crowded. On fine nights I walked to Cambridge, and carried my laundry, done at home. You see what a contrast that is to the present method of transporting thousands upon thousands of people every day, Sunday included, between Boston and Harvard Square and the populous districts lying beyond.

There was a noble elm tree which stood in the middle of Harvard Square. Here it is represented rather imperfectly. When that tree was cut down to make better room for the horse-cars, a lamentation went up from all the region round about, for it was a much-admired tree.

HARVARD SQUARE IN 1869

THE next picture is Harvard Square in 1869. You see that this is a distinctly later view, though it gives a similar impression of the rural, rustic nature of the Square.

Harvard Square in 1869

HARVARD COLLEGE, 1775

Showing Original Shape of Harvard Hall

Now we go back to Harvard College in 1775. On the right of the picture is Massachusetts Hall; on the left, Harvard. Let me call your attention to the fact that Harvard Hall, when first built, was a much better-looking building than it is now, or was in the eighteen-forties, fifties, and sixties. It had no rectangular projection in the middle of the front. Again, Massachusetts appears to great advantage, and there is a tolerably clear indication of the shield at the western end of the upper story, which has recently been replaced. The costumes of the personages in the front are supposed to be rather accurately represented; you observe that several of them carry canes for decorative purposes, a custom which has lately come in again. These, however, are not photographs, and we cannot be sure that they are correct representations.

Harvard College in 1775

HARVARD HALL WITH STUDENTS, 1860

This is the Harvard Hall which contains the rectangular
projection in the middle of the front. That ugly job was done
in President Quincy's time, I do not know by what architect;
but it seemed to President Quincy and the graduates of that
time a work of necessity. The original hall was divided into
three rooms on the lower story; the second story was carried on
brick partitions, and there was no large room on either story.
The College did not own a room capable of seating a large
number of persons at dinner, for example, on Commencement
Day. For such uses a large hall was needed, where four, five,
six, or eight hundred persons could assemble. Now, President
Quincy, meeting this necessity, took out all the partitions that
supported the second floor of Harvard Hall and its roof and
cupola, and replaced those partitions with tall, plain iron pillars or posts. To carry the superposed weight, there had to be
a great many of them; so that, when people stepped into this
really spacious room, what struck them most was the forest of
iron pillars. The group of students exhibited in this picture —

Harvard Hall in 1860

I suppose they were students assembled on Commencement or some other special day — are not dressed like the students of to-day. See how many of them wear tall silk hats. Some of those sitting in the windows have a less formal aspect; but on the whole this is, from our point of view, an amusing assemblage of students. Our ideas change from generation to generation.

HARVARD HALL, 1872

THE next is a picture of Harvard Hall in later times. In 1870 or 1871 new uses for Harvard Hall presented themselves. The Corporation had converted Massachusetts Hall from student chambers into two stories of large rooms, the upper room having the whole area of the hall, and one large room and one small room being provided in the lower story. We had acquired, that is to say, a hall big enough for the largest college assemblies at that time, and no longer needed the very ugly room in Harvard Hall. Moreover, we had need of more lecture-rooms, — an urgent need, — and indeed it seemed as if that was the greatest need of the College at that moment. So the Corporation directed Ware and Van Brunt to cut up again the lower story of Harvard into separate rooms, and hoped that they would succeed in enlarging the lower-story rooms. This is their design for that purpose. It certainly was a great departure from the original Harvard Hall, with its simple rectangular plan; but the design I think is much more pleasing than was the preceding design of President Quincy's time with its

Harvard Hall in 1872

unsightly projection on the front. This building has served its purpose very well now for fifty years, more than fifty years, and it bids fair to survive a good many years more, for it serves permanent needs well. You notice the round-headed windows which were used in the Harvard Hall of 1766, and later in University Hall, by Thomas Bulfinch, sometimes called the first American architect.

HOLWORTHY HALL IN 1859 AND 1878

I NOW present a pair of pictures of Holworthy Hall. Of
course this was a degenerate building as compared with Hollis.
Both design and construction are inferior. Students of architecture will have noticed that there is a greater space between
the caps of the windows in the upper story and the cornice, in
the second view than in the first. That change might be called
an investment on the part of the President and Fellows. The
rooms had been very low, hardly six feet and a half in the clear,
inside. By this change they were made a good height and
commanded a larger rent than they had before. The Corporation, I fear, had in view the money advantage rather than the
improvement of the aspect of the building; but its looks were
certainly greatly improved.

I want to say a word or two about the quality of the College
dormitories as a whole. There were no dormitories outside the
Yard except the building called College House across the
Square, the lower story used for shops; and that had been part
of the motive of the Corporation in building this structure —
that they might have some shops to let to Cambridge trades-

Holworthy Hall in 1859

Holworthy Hall in 1878

men, and also a fine corner to let to the Cambridge Bank, where the College authorities kept all their accounts and where most of the Cambridge residents connected with the University kept their accounts. It was a service to the bank that they hoped to render. Next door to the bank was the only savings bank at that time, which was a place of meeting for most of its directors, who there obtained pleasant access to the morning newspaper and conversation. The upper stories of College House were used entirely for students' rooms — small rooms and noisy according to the standards of that day. Of course it was not noise in the present sense. The rooms were used for the accommodation of students who could not afford to hire a room inside the Yard. The rents of all these rooms were very low, and the accommodations were extremely simple; so were the accommodations provided in the Yard itself extremely simple. It was a tremendous event when a sewer was built across the College Yard. It did not work very well, but it replaced cesspools, which were used by the students, who brought pails of dirty water from their rooms.

In the evening there were no lights in the Yard in my time as a student; no lights at all. I had the satisfaction of introducing gas into the College Yard, but at first into only one dormitory, Holworthy. I wanted gas in my room, Holworthy 11, very much; so I went to the President, James Walker, and asked him if I might be allowed to approach the Cambridge Gas Company, then in its beginnings, to suggest that it would be a good investment for them to put gas-pipes, as well as meters, into the rooms in Holworthy Hall. The first answer I got from the President was an absolute refusal. He said that it would be very dangerous; for the students would play all sorts of pranks with the gas, and they would also do damage through neglect, leave gas-cocks open, and blow up the building. But I was rather persistent, and went again, and finally President Walker agreed that I should sound the President of the Cambridge Gas Company on the subject of putting into Holworthy not only the meters in every room, but the piping itself. I found that the President of the Gas Company immediately looked with considerable favor on this suggestion; and it was not long before he notified me that his company was prepared to do just that thing. At the present moment the gas-piping in that Hall belongs to the Cambridge Gas Company, unless they have lost their rights by lapse of time. No harm came from this introduction of gas, and before long — two or three years — gas was introduced into all the College dormitories. Later some gas lamps were put up in the College Yard itself, to light it when the moon was not shining.

The Harvard Yard and Buildings

I remember an illustration of the difficulties in administering college discipline, which resulted from the darkness of the Yard. One night I was reading in my room in Hollis, when suddenly I heard a tremendous uproar in the Yard — screaming and shouting, yelling, and occasionally a burst of song, though but little of that, for at that time few students sang. But what was this noise? I ran down into the Yard and saw dimly that a procession was just passing the end of Massachusetts, a turbulent procession heading toward Hollis. At that time the amiable and altogether delightful Professor Child was Chairman of the Parietal Committee. I believe that name still survives for the Committee comprising all the instructors having rooms in the College buildings and all proctors.

I headed at once for Professor Child's room, Holworthy 11; but before I got half-way there, I met Professor Child himself. He exhibited considerable indignation. He first asked me what this riot was. I did not know. "Mr. Eliot, they are passing by Hollis this minute. They are heading out of the Yard through the posts near Holworthy. Go to the head of the procession and stop it, and disperse it."

An awkward job that seemed, but I hastened to the head of the procession, arriving just as it was going out of the Yard into the street. There was one gas-light already set up in the street

outside, not very far off. It did not do me any good. I was
then, as now, extremely nearsighted, and found it very difficult
to recognize people even in the day-time in the street, or on
the paths in the Yard, and an impossibility at night. But I
was then instructing the Sophomore Class, and I soon heard
voices at the head of the procession that I recognized; and
finally I heard a stammering student, with whose enunciation
I was familiar, say, "Hullo, fellers, I guess we'd better go
home. Old Eliot's round."

The title "old" amused me, even at that moment. I was
about twenty. I informed that student that he had better go
home; and the news spread. I recognized other voices, and
advised them to go home, and the result was that the procession was really broken up. It turned out to be the product of
a meeting held in Dane Hall (now disappeared; it stood facing
the Square near the southerly end of Matthews, right on the
street). Many law students and undergraduates had assembled
in the large lecture-room of Dane Hall to greet the "great
American traveller," Daniel Pratt, a half-crazy fellow who
often amused the unthinking part of the American public in
the middle years of the nineteenth century by his boastful
talk of personal adventure.

That illustrates the condition of the Yard in those days,

and also the manners and customs of law students and undergraduates.

I have already mentioned that there was no sewer at that time in the Yard — or only a feeble one, competent to carry off surface-water only. The town as a whole had no sewerage system. In the days of which I am now speaking, 1849–59, there was no water-supply in the College Yard. In fact, the Cambridge Water Company was new, and gave an imperfect service to only a few of the streets of Cambridge. You see what was involved in that lack of a water-supply. The students in my time — nineteen twentieths of them — brought their water in their own pails from one of the two pumps in the Yard, carrying it up to their rooms themselves. They had no hot water whatever, unless they heated a pot on their own fire, and very few did that. Consequently the amount of bathing done in the College was extremely limited. A few students employed men who came to their rooms at anywhere from three to five o'clock in the morning, and blacked boots, tended the fires, and brought up the coal from the cellar; but to have an attendant of that kind was unusual in the College buildings.

These deficiencies in comfort and the means of healthy living remained a long time after 1850, and only gradually disappeared. I remember, for instance, when the first bath-tubs were introduced, in the early years of my presidency. They were put into the cellar of Matthews Hall when it was built and they were the first on the College premises. The building of the Hemenway Gymnasium later, with its ample plumbing, caused the tubs in Matthews to be abandoned. They have been taken out since, I understand; but all the dormitories now have running water, and you can hardly imagine how great an improvement that has made in the manners and customs of Harvard students.

UNIVERSITY HALL, 1823

H ERE is the great architectural effort of the College in the early part of the nineteenth century, the building of University Hall (1812–13). It was a structure of white granite, the best granite that has ever been discovered in this vicinity — the quarries are no longer worked. Here is Bulfinch's design of University Hall, and shows it as originally constructed. You see there was a sort of piazza along the front, connecting the two entrance doors, and over it a roof. I never saw that roof myself. Most architects regard the removal as an improvement. The first story of University Hall contained four rooms just like the one which now exists at its southerly end. Four — one for each of the College classes — and "Commons" were provided there, the bakery and kitchen being in the well-lighted basement. "Commons," or common meals for students, have always given the College officers trouble, and been sources of discontent and disorder among the students. The manners and customs at Commons in this new University Hall surely left something to be desired. I remem-

University Hall in 1823

ber Mr. Francis B. Crowninshield, Harvard A.B. 1829, who was a member of the Corporation from 1861 to 1877, telling me that, as meat was hardly ever served at the supper table, he resorted to getting an extra slice of meat at dinner, which slice he pinned to the under-side of the table with his fork at his usual seat, so that it would be ready for him at supper. It was in one of these rooms in University, where bread-throwing was very active at times, that William H. Prescott, the historian of Spanish America, lost an eye. In 1849 Commons had become so troublesome that they were abolished by President Jared Sparks — by one of the first orders of his administration. And still common meals for students in large numbers remain a source of anxiety for Harvard administrators, in spite of Memorial Hall, the Harvard Union, and the Freshman dormitories.

WADSWORTH HOUSE, 1885

Next comes a picture of Wadsworth House. That to my eyes is one of the best of the College buildings. As I think I have already mentioned, it was built by the Colonial Legislature in 1726–27 for the new President of the College, Rev. Dr. Benjamin Wadsworth, pastor of the First Church of Boston; and the design, I suppose, was a standard one in those days. The form of fence was common then about good houses in Cambridge. The posts of this fence were of wood; but the regular College fence, parts of which still remain about the College Yard, had stone posts instead of wooden posts, and was more dignified than this. The Yard fence with stone posts was imitated in a considerable number of old towns in Massachusetts. It began at Harvard College, and is still held in honor.

Wadsworth House in 1885

BOYLSTON HALL BEFORE ALTERATION

This picture shows the original form of Boylston Hall. You see it is a pretty good-looking building. I cannot say that of the present Boylston Hall, which we shall see next. The original building had a good roof. How was that building spoiled? What led to the spoiling? Simply the growth of instruction in chemistry in Harvard College. In the original Boylston Hall, chemistry and mineralogy occupied rather more than half the space. The collections of the Peabody Museum, now on Divinity Avenue, occupied for many years a large fourth of the building, and the laboratory and lecture-room of Professor Jeffries Wyman the rest of it. Professor Wyman for many years had charge of the Peabody collections. But the Department of Chemistry developed so rapidly at Harvard under the leadership of Professor Josiah P. Cooke, aided by two remarkable assistant professors, — afterwards Professors Charles Loring Jackson and Henry Barker Hill, — that chemistry before long acquired the whole of Boylston Hall, that is, the whole of both the original stories. At the same time the laboratory

Boylston Hall in 1860

method of teaching chemistry and physics, rather than by lectures and recitations, was adopted by the Departments of both Chemistry and Physics. The need of laboratories for physics was met by the building of the Jefferson Physical Laboratory; but chemistry had no such benefactor as T. Jefferson Coolidge, so the chemical laboratories had to be supplied in Boylston Hall where the development of the instruction had gone on.

BOYLSTON HALL AFTER ALTERATION

THE only way to supply the pressing need seemed to be to put that hideous third story on Boylston Hall. This was the apology for the damage wrought to a dignified and solid building, the original design of which was not bad.

Boylston Hall in 1885

GORE HALL, 1844

HERE is a sad case of a building which has absolutely disappeared, having been taken down, and the materials carted away, in spite of the fact that it bore the name of Christopher Gore, eminent citizen, governor, and the largest benefactor the College had ever had ($95,000) in 1831. This is the building as it was originally built in 1839–42. Its construction was regarded as a great achievement by the College in the eighteen-forties. It was warmly welcomed by the graduates as affording in its nave a dignified place of gathering on Commencement Day and other festive occasions. When Cambridge became a city, Gore Hall was placed on its seal. Let me call your attention to the fact that the towers and the pinnacles on the buttresses are long and thin in this picture, longer and higher than they were in the eighteen-fifties. It happened that two or three times tall, thin stones from these towers fell out; fortunately in each case they fell to the ground, and did not go down through the building. Examination showed that the towers and pinnacles

Gore Hall in 1844

were unsafe; so that they had to be taken down and rebuilt, shorter but secure. Here we have another instance of bad work in masonry or bricklaying, compelling in a comparatively few years extensive repairs on a college building. Not only did it become necessary to repair the stone-work of Gore Hall, but also to introduce a new heating apparatus. The original heating apparatus was invented by Daniel Treadwell, Rumford Professor of the Application of Science to the Useful Arts (1834–45), and was a memorable piece of pioneer work in a subject which has since received a tremendous development. It was a low-pressure steam-heat system, the radiators for which were very tall and large, and built of large copper tubes soldered together. These tubes, however, were apt to leak steam, in consequence of which the atmosphere of the library became charged with aqueous vapor, and this vapor condensed, not only on the windows in the colder seasons of the year, but also on the books themselves. This defect ultimately led to the complete reconstruction of the heating apparatus of Gore Hall.

GORE HALL, 1878

Soon after I became President, it appeared that there was not room enough in Gore Hall for the proper storage of the books or for proper reading and catalogue rooms. An addition was, therefore, planned on the easterly side. That addition contained the first steel stack for books ever constructed. It preceded by a good many years the stacks of the Congressional Library and of the Boston Public Library, and on the whole it was admirably designed and executed by Messrs. Ware and Van Brunt. Now it has all gone. Why? Because, again, the University began to feel the lack of adequate space for the storage of its great collections of books, of reading-rooms for students, and of studies for professors. Widener Hall has provided it with all those things, and particularly it has provided space for some of the professional libraries lately bought in Europe by the University. The new School of Business Administration has valuable provision in Widener Hall for its growing and very useful professional library. The Department

Gore Hall in 1878

of History has admirable accommodations for its collections, and also for some private collections belonging to its professors. When Widener Hall had been planned and was assured, Gore Hall was doomed. It was beyond question desirable to have the principal library of the University secure in a really fire-proof building. Gore Hall lent itself to no other uses. This is another case of the failure of a College building to survive as a monument.

This is one of the subjects to which architects and landscape architects alike ought, I think, to give close attention for the future, the immediate future as well as the remote. What is a monument? What ought it to be? Ought it to be any structure or building, which has uses? Is that the right idea for a monument? Personally I think not, and I have recently testified to that effect before the Committee which has under consideration what they shall recommend to the Massachusetts Legislature in the way of a monument to the soldiers in the World War, more particularly to those from Massachusetts who died in that War. I believe that the real monuments and the surviving monuments are structures of high architectural and artistic merit which have no uses whatever. The most perfect monument I know on the surface of our earth is the Washington Monument at Washington, the most perfect in form and in sentiment, and therefore the most likely to endure. Of course we can all think of famous monuments in Europe, Asia, and Egypt which have these same qualities of beauty, dignity, and inspiration, and therefore have lasted, and will last. For endowed universities this subject of durable monuments to benefactors seems to me to have much significance.

PRESIDENT ELIOT'S HOUSE, 1875

Tʜɪs former President's house is another illustration of failure to make a durable monument to a considerable giver. Mr. Peter C. Brooks, father-in-law of Edward Everett, who was President from 1846 to 1849, conceived the idea that there ought to be a substantial, good-looking, and well-arranged President's house in the College grounds. He gave a considerable sum in 1846 for the construction of such a house; but his son-in-law, Edward Everett, served as President for only three years, and then retired to his own house on Summer Street, Boston. The next President, Jared Sparks, already owned a very desirable house at the corner of Quincy and Kirkland Streets, from which he refused to be detached. So the Peter C. Brooks Fund was left to accumulate for a time. In 1860, this substantial house was built, and occupied for a short time by President Felton. Then President Hill and his family lived in it for seven years; but it was then the scene of much sickness and sorrow.

From the autumn of 1869, I lived in that house for forty

President Eliot's House
1875

years. It was hot in summer, because the second story of the house, which contained the principal chambers, had a curved slated wall. Those slates absorbed on a summer day much heat, which remained long after sunset; so that the second- and third-story rooms were intolerable in summer. I procured some changes in the lower story which made it convenient for company occasions; and its site and surroundings were always very agreeable. Mr. Brooks's gift disappeared twelve years ago. It has gone forever. President Lowell wished to give the University a larger and better President's house, but essentially on the same site. He did so.

I hope that as architects and landscape architects you will keep in mind this doctrine of the worthy monument, and the desirableness of commemorating in lasting ways the benevolent men and women who give of their private fortunes for public uses. If the American public can be prevented from impetuously putting up ill-considered and inartistic monuments, you may have good chances to design during the next twenty years durable memorials to great public characters, and to large numbers of heroic men who in the World War gave their lives to win for mankind justice, good-will, and peace.

Made in the USA
Charleston, SC
05 June 2013